Beginner Biography

Sequoyah
Man of Many Words

by Jeri Cipriano
illustrated by Scott R. Brooks

Red Chair Press   Egremont, Massachusetts

Look! Books are produced and published by Red Chair Press:

Red Chair Press LLC   PO Box 333   South Egremont, MA 01258-0333

www.redchairpress.com

FREE lesson guide at www.redchairpress.com/free-activities

Publisher's Cataloging-In-Publication Data

Names: Cipriano, Jeri S., author. | Brooks, Scott R., illustrator.

Title: Sequoyah : man of many words / by Jeri Cipriano ; illustrated by Scott R. Brooks.

Description: Egremont, Massachusetts : Red Chair Press, [2020] | Series: Look! books. Beginner biography | Includes index, glossary, and resources for further reading. | Interest age level: 006-009. | Summary: "As a young Cherokee man, Sequoyah had a voice. He liked to talk, but he could not write his words to share with others. He decided to make symbols for every sound in his language. His work allowed the Cherokee people to survive many challenges"--Provided by publisher.

Identifiers: ISBN 9781634409810 (library hardcover) | ISBN 9781634409827 (paperback) | ISBN 9781634409834 (ebook)

Subjects: LCSH: Sequoyah, 1770?-1843--Juvenile literature. | Cherokee Indians--Biography--Juvenile literature. | Cherokee language--Alphabet--Juvenile literature. | Cherokee language--Writing--Juvenile literature. | CYAC: Sequoyah, 1770?-1843. | Cherokee Indians--Biography. | Cherokee language.

Classification: LCC E99.C5 S3821 2020 (print) | LCC E99.C5 (ebook) | DDC 975.004/97557/0092 B--dc23

Library of Congress Control Number : 2019940525

Photo credits: p. 20: Luc Novovitch/Alamy; p. 20: National Geographic Image Collection/Alamy; p. 20: Dennis MacDonald/Alamy; p. 21: Architect of the Capitol; p. 21: Caleb Long

Printed in the United States of America

0420 1P CGF20

Table of Contents

A Big Idea

Suppose you make a new friend. You can give each other your names and phone numbers. You know how to write the letters of your name.

Years ago, Cherokee (CHER-o-key) people did not have a way to write their language. Without an **alphabet**, people cannot read nor write.

One man changed that. His name was Sequoyah (se-KOY-uh). Sequoyah decided to **invent** a way to write the Cherokee language!

Sequoyah

Sequoyah was born around 1778. He made things from silver. Other **silversmiths** signed their work. Sequoyah wished he could write his name, too.

In the town where he lived, Sequoyah saw white men looking at sheets of paper with marks all over them. The white men could make sounds from the marks. He called these papers "talking leaves."

Good to Know

Many of the Cherokee thought these talking leaves were magic. Sequoyah knew it was a way to read the white man's language.

Making a Way to Write

Sequoyah wanted to make "talking marks" too. He drew small pictures for everything he saw. A picture of a tree stood for the word *tree*. A picture of a bird stood for the word *bird*.

Years went by. Finally, Sequoyah gave up. It was taking too long to draw pictures for every word he knew.

A System That Works

Sequoyah needed a new idea. Then it came to him. He would make up **symbols** to stand for sounds he heard.

Sequoyah made up 85 symbols. He had a symbol for every sound in his language.

Good to Know

Sequoyah's list of symbols that stand for each sound in the language is called a syllabary. In our language today each sound in a word is a **syllable** or part of the word.

The symbols stand for sounds in the Cherokee language.

The First Student

Sequoyah taught his daughter how to say and write each symbol.

Then he wrote a few symbols. His daughter said the word. He wrote different symbols. She said a new word. His daughter was reading Cherokee!

Good to Know

English is harder to learn than Cherokee. Our letters stand for more than one sound. Say hop. Now say hope. Which letter has two different sounds?

Sequoyah's daughter was named Ayoka.

Show and Tell

Sequoyah taught more young people. Then in 1821, they went to see the tribal leaders. The children showed what they could do with the symbols.

The leaders were surprised. Now there was a way to write down the history of their people.

Success for Sequoyah

The leaders thanked Sequoyah. They gave him a **medal**. He never took it off.

About 7 years later, Sequoyah helped start a newspaper. It had news in English and Cherokee. People read it all across the Cherokee nation. Sequoyah also helped write the Cherokee peoples' **Constitution.**

From 1838 to 1839, the Cherokee and other tribes were forced by the U.S. government to move to a new place. It was important that the Cherokee had language to tie them together.

Good to Know

In 1838, the Cherokee and other tribes were forced to walk hundreds of miles to Indian Territory. Thousands died along this Trail of Tears.

Timeline: Big Dates in Sequoyah's Life

1778: Sequoyah is born in Tennessee; the date is not known for sure.

1812: War of 1812 begins.

1813: Sequoyah joins the Army with other Native soldiers.

1814: He returns home from the Army.

1815: Sequoyah marries Sally Watters.

1821: He shows his written language to tribal leaders.

1824: Sequoyah is given a medal of honor for his invention.

1828: He travels to Washington D.C. with other leaders to sign a treaty.

1829: He settles in Indian Territory, part of today's Oklahoma.

1838: The Cherokee tribe is moved by force to Indian Territory.

1843: While searching for Cherokee who moved there, Sequoyah dies in Mexico.

The Cherokee People Today

Festivals are still held today in Cherokee, NC.

Cherokee elders keep traditions alive by sharing them with children.

Cherokee crafts are kept alive today in Georgia, North Carolina, and Oklahoma.

In 1917, the state of Oklahoma gave a statue of Sequoyah to stand in the U.S. Capitol building. It was the first statue to honor a Native American.

The Cherokee Nation Courthouse in Tahlequah, Oklahoma served as the tribal capital from 1869 to 1907 when Oklahoma became a state.

Good to Know

One Cherokee tradition is never to say good-bye. Instead, they have a word that means "until we meet again."

Words to Know

alphabet: a set of letters (A–Z) or marks used to write a language

Constitution: the beliefs and laws of a group

invent: make something that did not exist before

medal: an award given to show respect

silversmith: a person who makes things from metal and silver

syllable: the different parts, or sounds, that make a word

symbol: a sign or mark that stands for something else

Learn More at the Library

(Check out these books to read with others)

Rumford, James. *Sequoyah: The Cherokee Man Who Gave His People Writing,* HMH Books for Young Readers, 2004.

Smith-Llera, Danielle. *The Cherokee: The Past and Present of a Proud Nation,* Capstone Press, 2015.

Strand, Jennifer. *Sequoyah (Native American Leaders),* Abdo Zoom, 2017.

Index

About the Author

Jeri Cipriano has written more than a hundred books for young readers. She enjoys reading and finding out new things. She likes to share what she learns.